WHY GOD HATES RELIGION

Written by

G. T. Harpazo

Illustrations by
©Vladimir Ceresnak | Dreamstime.com
Crows in a tree ID 24862867
Crows fly away from the tree ID 25806255

All scripture verses are taken from the King James Version
unless referenced otherwise.

"We are moving towards a completely religion-less age; people as they are now simply cannot be religious anymore. Even those who honestly describe themselves as 'religious' do not in the least act up to it. So they presumably mean something quite different by 'religious.'"

Dietrich Bonhoeffer-1944

Table of Contents

FOREWORD

HOW THIS BOOK WAS WRITTEN

This book has been in my head and my heart for a long, long time. I knew God wanted me to write this book, but I procrastinated. I wondered if this message was ready to be given or whether it would be timely considering the state of the Church. I have been a Christian for many years, taught the Scriptures, been a church leader and suffered religious and spiritual abuse.

But one day, God in His mercy delivered my wife and me from religion. I say "delivered" because it was not a mental decision, but a supernatural deliverance by God's Spirit. The first thing I noticed after this experience is that my Christian witness seemed to explode compared to how I was received by the world while being religious. I don't think it was my smile; attitude or anything else other than the Holy Spirit could shine forth now without a religious mask that hid the Light.

While enjoying this "liberty and freedom" in the Spirit, my wife and I noticed that sinners were attracted to the spiritual fruit without the judgmental attitude. We also noticed that we were immediately misunderstood by our religious friends. My mother-in-law who lived next door to us found it necessary to apologize to the religious folks for our change. She was obviously embarrassed by us and didn't know how to explain us.

Oddly enough, we could not adequately explain ourselves either. So we did what we always do.....we prayed. We had regular prayer meetings with family and friends in our home where we prayed for the lost and other needs. While we prayed in secret, God was working openly on my mother-in-law. One day she drove into the driveway from a church service and as she went to turn the key of her car, she blurted out, "That wasn't worth getting dressed for!" This was not from a backslidden woman, but a pastors' wife of almost thirty years.

God not only delivered her from religion, but she became a fiery witness to all who would listen. She became a bold witness on the street, in the stores and on the doorsteps of the public school.

This is a woman who feared speaking all the years she was a pastor's wife. On one occasion, she met a woman who had known her previously and asked the question, "Where are you going to church?" My mother-in-law began to speak and although I don't know what she said, by the time she got finished a crowd had gathered and was listening to every word. This was outside a school, not in a church building.

It reminded me of Jesus witnessing to the crowds outside, among the hills and byways and by the sea. Jesus got kicked out of the synagogue early in His ministry, but His witness was just as powerful in the world. In fact, Jesus declared a new relationship with all those who hear His Word and do it. He called them His "brother, sister and mother" or His family.

We have been living and enjoying our Christian life and relationship with Jesus from the time we were delivered from dead works and religion. Christianity is not a religion, but a relationship. It is not an organization, but a living organism. He is the Good Shepard (Pastor) and we are the sheep of His pasture. As Christians, we don't belong to a denomination or church organization, but we belong to a heavenly family.

I wrote this book in hopes that others will see the evils of religion and come out from it. My earnest prayer is that you will yearn to be free in the liberty in which God has called all of us. A mighty transformation is about to happen in the Church. The veil over the church's eyes will once again be torn asunder and the glory of the Lord will be poured out on all Christians. A mighty witness will occur when religion is stripped away and sinners see the reality of the Living Christ in a living person.

May God open your eyes and heart as you read this book.

CHAPTER 1

WHEN THE SPIRIT OF GOD REALLY MOVED

Alan said, "Tell us the story about the "goat lady." I was sitting in Alan's kitchen surrounded by his family of four kids and Mary, his wife. I smiled as I realized Alan had his own special way of remembering these stories when God's spirit was poured out in a mighty supernatural way. All of Alan's family began laughing and moved in closer in hopes of hearing this story one more time.

In the mid 1970's, I attended a small church in Texas that came into being in a supernatural way. The building was originally an old house in major need of repair. A preacher had purchased the building and was attempting to renovate it. On the day that the building was to be leveled, the preacher found himself underneath the house, in the mud, during a rainstorm, praying for help. All the "volunteers" did not show up and he was left alone with his wife to do this job. He did not want to show his disappointment, so he asked his wife to stand in the middle of the house while he placed the jacks under the foundation. She was to watch a level and shout out when the bubble reached the center.

Before pulling the jacks out of the truck, the preacher crawled under the house more to find a place to cry and pray than to survey the foundation. He was sure God had told him to buy this building and start this church. As he cried out to God, the floor of the building began to shake and produce loud cracking noises. Fearful that the house was collapsing upon him, he crawled out and ran into the building to warn his wife. As he entered the large room where his wife was standing, she yelled, "That's it. That's it."

The shaking had stopped and the floor was perfectly level. God had leveled the building by Himself without any help from man. So began a series of miracles that lasted many years in this church. God's presence and power were so evident, that the little church had services seven nights a week. Many would come and not want to leave the building. There were many saved, delivered and healed there along with wonderful manifestations of the Spirit of God.

We met Alan and Mary in Marietta, Georgia in the late 1980's where we pastored a small, store-front church named Grace and Glory Worship Center. They stayed in touch with us long after they moved back to Texas and raised their family. We loved visiting them and their family and this was one of those visits.

The "goat lady" was a lady named Sister Cox and she had nothing to do with goats. She was a sweet, elderly lady in the little church in Texas. She loved to testify of God's goodness every night we had services. Her testimony was always the same. How God saved her from a horrific car accident, healed her body and saved her soul. Many in the church knew this testimony by heart because they heard it every night, but the way she would tell it was so full of love and gratitude, that I always loved hearing it.

During the service, while we were praising and worshiping the Lord, a wave of anointing would flow through the whole congregation and many would be overwhelmed by the power of God's presence. Sister Cox would often let out a loud "holler" and begin dancing in a circle. Many times she would end up lowering her head and running into a wall before collapsing on the floor. (I guess that is why Alan called her the "goat lady.")

I would pick her up after the service was over and place her in my car. I would then drive her to her apartment on the other side of town. Sometimes she would be awake, but sometimes we would have to lay her on the couch and tell her son to watch her. The next night she was awake and ready to go to church again. She loved the presence of the Lord.

What most people would see as a crazy old lady that maybe got her brains ocrambled in a car accident, I saw differently. I saw a precious saint of God that never tired of thanking Him for saving her. She was faithful in giving Him all the praise and all the glory for her life. Jesus was her life. Now when I sit in church services that don't allow any manifestation of God's Spirit, and with no response from God's people, I wonder who the crazy ones really are.

I found this little church after much prayer. I lived in Louisiana, a distance of more than 70 miles from the church in Texas. I had recently committed my whole life to God and was looking for a church to attend. God gave me a dream of a building with a front porch and windows and a door with an oval etched pattern in the glass. I looked all over the town where I lived and could not find the place. It was only after meeting another Christian at work that I was invited to the church in Texas.

The church building was converted from an old house. The parking lot was behind the church and I normally entered through the back door. One Sunday after a wonderful service, I left the church through the front door. As I turned and looked over my shoulder, I saw the same front porch and windows and door from my dream. The windows had been covered by paneling from the inside. I knew at that moment that this was the church in my dream.

My experiences in this church were so dynamic and powerful, that I drove the 140 mile distance every night to attend services. I eventually moved to Texas and commuted the same distance to work so I could be closer to the church family. Eventually, God gave me a good job in Texas to end my commute. It has been many years since I have seen God move in the way He did in the church in Texas. The miracles and outpourings of His Spirit were so plentiful that we thought they would never stop. But one day, we realized God wasn't moving the same way He had before. Sadly, we had taken the moving of the Spirit for granted and perhaps had made a religion out of what had happened there.

Sometimes, we find ourselves doing the same things we did, the last time the Spirit moved, in hopes that God would do it again. Unfortunately, once we figure out how God works, He seldom works that way again. For example, in the 1970's, women came to church in skirts, sometimes in mini-skirts. Often the power and presence of God would cause men and women to fall out under the power. To prevent any embarrasoment to the women, the ladies of the church would place a sheet over the legs of those who had fallen down. Years later, when many women wore pants to church, the ladies were still placing sheets over those who had fallen under the power. They had made a religion out of this experience. Even the men received sheets. Some services resembled a morgue with bodies all over the floor and sheets covering them.

I remember one night when God was moving in a powerful way, a policeman knocked on the front door of the church. He had received a call from our neighbor – an alcoholic – that we were disturbing him. As the policeman entered the sanctuary, he took one look at the bodies littered on the floor and began stuttering and backing up toward the door. He politely asked us to hold it down and quickly left. Later the church would buy this neighbor's house and turn it into a home for the pastor.

There were many, many stories we told Alan, Mary and others about that time when God's Spirit moved. My wife and I are both writing books about those experiences, so I will not repeat them at this time. My prayer is that God would once again move in the power of His Spirit and His people would be able to receive all the spiritual manifestations that true praise and worship brings.

In order for this to happen, I believe the Church must change. She is the Bride of Christ waiting for His soon return. It is time for her to make herself ready to receive Him. Religion has robbed the Church of her purity and she has left her first love. The day will come when the Church will not be run like a business, nor will Church and money be synonymous. The Spirit of the Lord will be given the liberty to move any way He wants and the flesh will be powerless to stop Him. The result will be a glorious Church that Jesus desires when he returns. It will be a dynamic, supernatural body of believers that will do miracles, signs and wonders in His Name.

Now, the title of this book may have shocked you or maybe struck a chord in your heart. After all, you are reading it this far. Please stay with me and find out what I have learned about religion and how harmful it has been to Christianity and the church. I will attempt to define religion as we know it today. I love Jesus Christ and his church very much, but I believe the diversion of religion has from the beginning of time robbed the church of its power and witness. Many horrible things have been done in this world in the name of religion and continue to this day. Let's talk about religion and find out what God has to say about it.

CHAPTER 2

WHAT IS RELIGION?

As a Bible teacher, I look to the scriptures to explain why I think God hates religion. Some of this teaching may be new to you and if you have never read the Bible before, I encourage you to get one and read these scriptures for yourselves. Pray that the Holy Spirit (who inspired the Bible) will help you to understand. The Holy Spirit and the Bible are "two witnesses" that always agree. "By the mouth of two or three witnesses, (let) every word be established." (Matthew 18:16) May God establish His Word in your hearts.

"RELIGION...WHERE DID THIS WORD ORIGINATE?"

The Merriam-Webster dictionary states the word "religion" dates back to a 13th century Latin word "religare" meaning "to restrain, to tie back." The Bible has only a few verses that use the word "religion."

These verses are Acts 17:22, 25:19 and 26:5, Gal. 1:13 and James 1:26-27.

In the 17th chapter of the book of Acts, Paul stood in the midst of Mars' hill, and said, **Ye men of Athens, I perceive that in all things ye are too "superstitious!"** [deisidaimonesteros -- meaning "religious"]. If you break down the original text further, you find the word is from deilos -- which is from deos meaning dread or timid and by implication – faithless. The King James Version (KJV) translates this word as fearful. The second part of the word comes from daimon -- meaning a demon or supernatural spirit (of a bad nature). The KJV translates this word as devil.   Acts 25:19 also uses the same Greek word which is translated "superstition" in KJV and refers to religious beliefs.   In Acts 26:5 and Gal. 1:13, Paul refers to how his involvement in religion caused him to persecute the Church.

So the Bible interprets "religious" the same as "superstitious" and calls it a demonic spirit that causes us to be timid, fearful, full of dread and faithless.   **Did you get that? The Bible actually calls religion a superstitious practice inspired by the devil that**

17

leaves us fearful and faithless! Wow! That should open some of your eyes. We will see other proofs in the Bible that this evil practice has actually caused the Church to be persecuted and misled. This same religious spirit caused Cain to murder his brother Abel and led Paul to murder the early Christians thinking he was doing God a favor.

That was a hard pill to swallow! When I first began looking for references to religion in the Bible, I was surprised to find very little. Most of these references were very negative. I was shocked to find the word "religion" meant something very different than what most people perceive it to be today. Please don't turn me off because of your past perceptions, but go with me and let the Bible speak for itself.

"WELL, ISN'T CHRISTIANITY A RELIGION?"

Some may say, "Well, isn't Christianity a religion? The answer is NO! Christianity is a "relationship" with Jesus Christ. It is different from all religions in that it is based on a finished work of redemption by Christ on the cross and ratified by God who raised Jesus from the dead. So now, Christians are "In Christ", a part of His body, called the Church. This body, the Church, is a living organism, not an organized religion. No other religion can say that about its founder or can experience this oneness with God. Other religions ask their disciples to die for their God, but in Christianity, God died for His disciples. Christianity is more than a ceremonial observance; it is a transformation of the disciple into a "new creature." It is not reformation or ritual, but an ongoing revelation of Jesus Christ.

Obviously, Paul's use of the word "religion" is compared to being superstitious and implies a fearful, faithless attitude inspired by the devil. That's not a very attractive definition! I asked God: **"Are there any good uses of the word religion in the Bible?"** He led me to one positive use of the word "religion" in James 1:27. James states "Pure religion and undefiled before God and the Father is this...To visit the fatherless and widows in their affliction, and to keep himself unspotted from the world." The word "religion" in this verse is from the Greek threskeia -- and it means ceremonial observance or religion. This is external religious worship or religion that is expressed in outward acts.

A closer look at the original text finds "to visit" the fatherless and widows means to "visit, help and care for them." We see examples of this type of religion in the 6th Chapter of Acts where the "twelve" chose "seven men of honest report, full of the Holy Ghost and wisdom" to attend to the task of caring for the widows. They referred to this ministry as "serving tables." One of these men was Steven who "full of faith and power, did great wonders and miracles among the people" and became the first Christian martyr. Another waiter of tables was Phillip who after witnessing to the Ethiopian eunuch on the Gaza road, was translated "caught away" [harpazo – rapture] and was found later 20 miles away. This example of servant-hood led to the ministry and growth of the early church.

My wife and I got to experience this type of "pure religion" for a period of several years. After pastoring a church in Georgia, God led me to go back to a place that I definitely didn't want to go. Not only had I experienced a lot of religious abuse in this place, but I believed God was the one who told me to leave "shaking the dust off my feet." I guess I had some areas of my heart that needed more breaking and cleansing. I didn't know there was bitterness hidden deep in my heart.

Shortly after arriving back in "Egypt", all hell broke loose. Every day led to hardship and loss. It was definitely a test of obedience. The good news was that my former pastor (who was also my father-in-law), called my wife and I to stand before his congregation and publicly apologized for all the harm and hurt he had done to us. We were reconciled and forgiveness flowed. Two weeks later, this pastor died in a tragic automobile accident. We knew there had been a purpose for our return. God allowed us to give and receive forgiveness and to heal this relationship prior to this pastor's untimely death

We were left with a church where we had ministered and been associate pastors for 14 years. This was a church that had lost their only senior pastor. Although the church asked us to be the new pastors, every service was a memorial to our senior pastor. The church never survived the loss. Too many churches are built around the personality and charisma of one pastor and can not accept anything new. This was the case with this small church in Texas. This church had seen many miracles, but had slowly died. It is difficult to see this happen. The church is not a building or a place, but we often associate God's presence with these things.

We all need to remember that the Lord is our Pastor (Shepherd). He will never leave us or forsake us. He is a 24-hour, 7-days-a-week Pastor. Our eyes should never be on sinful man, no matter how charismatic or faithful. My wife and I were used of God to lead most of the existing congregation to new church homes and the old church building was given to a new congregation which is still active today.

My experience with preachers has not always been a good one. I often found them to be somewhat arrogant and proud. They would always talk about the size of their churches or congregations in an attempt to "one-up" one another. They talked of the flock as their possessions instead of identifying with the sheep. When I asked them why they didn't fellowship with the flock, their answer was "Shepherds fellowship with shepherds and sheep fellowship with sheep." It was hard for me to distinguish these "men of God" from politicians who wear nice suits and shake hands in public and act completely different behind the scenes. I know not all preachers are like this, and there are many humble men and women of God who genuinely love the church.   But, be warned, not every religious person is what they are supposed to be.

My wife and I thought our job was done, but God had other plans. We moved out of our nice home and into a trailer park to be next to my widowed mother-in-law. This was somewhat of a pride-buster for me. However, we quickly learned that the people who inhabited the trailer park were a very diverse, friendly and needy group. Many of the children in the trailer park had single parents or "incapacitated" parents and were left to roam the street alone. As I worked on my small yard, many young boys would stand in the street and talk to me. They would eventually ask if they could help me pull weeds and do yard work. None of them asked for a reward or any pay. They just needed something to do and a friendly person to be with.

I recognized these "orphans" needed help, but I did not want them to come over to my house without their parent's permission. So I would follow them home and meet their parents. I would ask permission to let them come over to my yard. I made a point to not bring them into the house or allow them to do anything with me that would appear wrong. I realized the world we are living in holds a lot of evil and these children were so vulnerable to the wrong kind of adult. So we did what we could to love them, encourage them, and pray for them.

Once all the children in the trailer park were asked by my mother-in-law to sweep the park and pick up trash. The younger kids were excited to have something to do while the older kids were skeptical and just watched. My mother-in-law had the children line up on one side of the park and walk across the grassy infield. They were given plastic bags and picked up all the litter and trash in their path. When they reached the other side, my mother-in-law had them place their bags on the ground, turn around and observe their handiwork. They were amazed at how beautiful the once dirty area had become. The older kids were also impressed.

The same year, on Easter, we had an egg hunt for all the children in the park and gave each an Easter card with the message of Christ in language they could understand. The trailer park residents were a diverse group of people from Hispanic,

Vietnamese, Gay, African-American and other backgrounds. Many of the parents told us they read the Easter tract to their children and thanked us.

I "waited" on other widows in the park and did my best to help them when they needed it. Our trailer was newer and bigger than most and we became known as the rich folks up on "Knob Hill." Of course, we lived in a flat place and our home was not even on a hill, but the name stuck. We provided transportation and other help because many couldn't afford a car. Many would come by my mother-in-law's house to sit on the porch and hear her kind and loving words.

She was so beloved that she never worried about crime or harm while she lived there. When trouble would come (usually at 2 AM) and the police would show up (which is common in a trailer park), my mother-in-law would stand out in the street in her housecoat and tell the people to stop fighting and love one another. On one occasion, a very drunk person wanted to get in my mother-in-law's face and immediately, two very big men were standing next to her asking "Miss Billie" if she needed any help!

I was a little worried about her boldness and safety so I let it be known that "Miss Billie" was really in touch with the owner of the park and any infraction of their detailed lease agreements would result in immediate eviction. I asked God to forgive me for this "deliberate misunderstanding." The truth was the park had no manager. I reminded our neighbors that calling the police would only work for a few hours, but calling the park owner would be a much better deterrent. Because many of the neighbors had not read their lease agreement and did not know how much legal power the owner had over them, they quickly realized that being evicted and not being able to afford moving their trailer would result in the loss of their home. Police calls were greatly reduced and the park changed dramatically.

I believe this was an example of "pure religion" in action. On more than one occasion, I had the privilege of praying with sinners who approached me and wanted a relationship with Jesus Christ. All it takes is for the world to see the Living Christ in a living person to make them hungry for what we have been freely given…an abundant life. Our religious works will never attract the lost. "And I, if I (Jesus) be

lifted up from the earth, will draw all men unto me."
(John 12:32)

CHAPTER 3

WHAT ABOUT THE JEWISH RELIGION?

Didn't God create religion by giving Israel all those rules and regulations?

Again, the answer is NO! God gave Israel commandments to obey. Israel took 10 commandments and made over 400 rituals and regulations. Like all religions, man decides what rituals and regulations will allow us to please God. None of these religions involve hearing the voice of God for yourself without going through a sinful, human intermediary. It is interesting that Judaism's basic confession of faith is Deuteronomy 6:4 which begins with "Hear, O Israel." It is called the Shema which is from the word "Hear."

When Jesus was asked, "Master, which is the great commandment of the law?" in Matthew 23:36, He answered from Deuteronomy 6:9 (part of the Shema) and Leviticus 19:18. "Jesus said unto him, Thou shalt love the Lord thy God with all thy heart, and with all thy soul, and with all thy mind. This is the first and great commandment. And the second is like unto it, Thou shalt love thy neighbor as thyself. On these two commandments hang all the law and the prophets." He was the first to combine these two commandments into one summary of all of the law of the Jews.

Samuel asked Saul (1 Samuel 15: 22)..."Hath the Lord as great delight in burnt offerings and sacrifices, as in obeying the voice of the Lord? Behold, to obey is better than sacrifices, and to hearken than the fat of rams." Psalms 51:17 states..."The sacrifices of God are a broken spirit; a broken and contrite heart, O God, thou wilt not despise." This type of brokenness of heart and spirit will present itself to God as a "living sacrifice" (Romans 12:1) and a "sweet savour of Christ in them that are saved." So Christianity is based on hearing and obeying the word of God as "living sacrifices", not offerings of dead sacrifices to please God. Throughout the Bible, God presents Himself as a God of the Living, not of the dead. He repeatedly told Israel that disobedience and rebellion takes away life, but obedience brings life....an abundance of life.

In the book of Romans, Paul, the apostle, clearly teaches that those who place their trust in

Jesus Christ are not under the law. They are saved by grace through faith in Christ, and not the works of the law. Paul's concludes, "Therefore, being justified by faith" (not by works- Rom. 4:1-8; not by ordinances – Rom. 4:9-12, and not by obedience to the law – Rom. 4:13-25) "we have peace with God through our Lord Jesus Christ. By whom also we have access by faith into the grace wherein we stand and rejoice in hope of the glory of God." (Rom. 5:1-2) So the way to receive from God all that you need for an abundant life, and in the end, eternal life is "by grace through faith."

My wife and I have had the privilege to participate in many of the Jewish feasts and to study Jewish customs and traditions. What we found fascinating is that all of them contain symbols of Christianity including the Trinity, Jesus Christ and other "signs and wonders." We do not celebrate these feasts out of obligation or commandment, but it is a blessing to see God speak the hidden mysteries of His Word. When we pastored Grace and Glory Worship Center in Georgia, the only pastor that befriended us was a messianic Rabbi. He was filled with love and grace and opened his heart and church to us. The music and worship at this messianic church was wonderful. My wife is Jewish and although she was never a practicing Jew, she loved being reunited with her "roots."

CHAPTER 4

WHEN DID RELIGION BEGIN?

A good place to answer this question is to look in the Book of Beginnings – Genesis. We read in Chapter One the story of creation and how God created man and woman. "And God saw every thing that he had made, and, behold, it was very good. And the evening and the morning were the sixth day." "And God blessed the seventh day, and sanctified it: because that in it he had rested from all his work which God created and made." And Chapter two starts a new week with God. We learn in this chapter that God created an abundance of fruit trees in the Garden of Eden. He mentions two fruit trees by name...the "Tree of Life" and the "Tree of the Knowledge of Good and Evil." (Gen. 2:8)

Did religion begin when God created Adam and Eve?

No, because they were without sin and talked to God daily. They had no need of sacrifices and religious ritual to approach God.

Did religion originate with the slaying of animals by God to provide a sacrifice and clothing for Adam & Eve?

No, for God slew the animals to provide a covering for their nakedness. This sacrifice did not remove sin and restore their original relationship with God. God did not create religion. He has always wanted a relationship without man-made ritual and sacrifice. God is not religious.

Did religion originate with the eating of the fruit of the knowledge of good & evil?

No, this opened Adam & Eve to know good & evil, but knowing good & evil does not ensure man will choose good over evil. Man was created with a free will. We will see this later in Chapter 5 when we talk about the impact of eating this fruit.

For now, let's investigate what really happened in the garden of Eden. "And the LORD God planted a garden eastward in Eden; and there he put the man whom he had formed. And out of the ground made the LORD God to grow every tree that is pleasant to the sight, and good for food; the **tree of life** also in the midst of the garden, and the **tree of knowledge of good and evil.**"   (Gen. 2:8-9) "And the LORD God took the man, and put him into the garden of Eden to dress it and to keep it. And the LORD God commanded the man, saying, Of every tree of the garden thou mayest freely eat: But of the tree of the knowledge of good and evil, thou shalt not eat of it: for in the day that thou eatest thereof thou shalt surely die." (Gen.2:15-17)

So we see that God planted a garden, formed man from the dust, made him a "living soul", placed man in the garden and gave him a commandment about two specific trees in the garden. Afterward, God decided to create "woman" from the living flesh of Adam. So man and the animals were made of "hard dirt" and woman was made from the soft flesh of man. This is why Adam called her "Woman" which not only means "from man" but can also mean "to be soft." In chapters 1-5 of Genesis, God says a lot about Adam and Eve. He created them to be one flesh or one person, both in His image, both with dominion over all the earth, and both called by one name, Adam. (Gen. 1:26-31; 2:23-25; and 5:2) They were both spiritual beings, clothed in the glory of God so they did not need clothes and were not ashamed.

So what happened with Eve and the serpent? The serpent was made by God as a beautiful and very smart ("more clever") creature. Obviously, Satan who existed as a disembodied spirit on Earth chose this creature to possess because it had the capacity to communicate with man. It may be man and woman, in their higher state, had the ability to communicate with all the animals. We don't know. We do know that Satan was once an angel named Lucifer and was in Eden when it was a place filled with precious stones. He was corrupted by his beauty and wisdom and was destroyed because of his rebellion against God. (Ezekiel 28:13-19; Isaiah 14:12-23)

Let's look at the conversation between Satan and the Woman. "And he said to the woman, Yea, hath God said, Ye shall eat of every tree of the garden?" The Hebrew lexicon translates this question as "Is it even so, that God has said you shall eat of no tree in the garden?" The Woman responds with what she understands as the Word of God. "We may eat of the fruit of the trees of the garden. But of the fruit of the tree which is in the midst of the garden, God hath said, Ye shall not eat of it, **neither shall ye touch it**, lest ye die. And the serpent said unto the woman, Ye shall not surely die! For God doth know that in the day ye eat thereof, then your eyes shall be opened, and **ye shall be as gods, knowing good and evil."** (Gen. 3:2-3)

When we compare what the Woman claims "God hath said", we notice something different about God's commandment. Did God say that Adam and Eve could not touch the fruit?   God did say it was "pleasant to the sight and good for food." But in Gen. 2, God never said you couldn't touch it.   Where did Eve get this information?   Well, obviously, she was not even created when God told Adam the commandment about the trees of the garden.   So Adam must have told Eve what God had said.   And as man is prone to do, he added an extra word to the commandment because he either did not trust Eve or he thought he was being more attentive than God.

This is where I believe religion was started. It was started by a man named Adam and led to the fall of mankind. In its purest definition, religion is created when man adds to or takes away from the Word of God. Adam added to the word of God when he told Eve not to touch the fruit or she would die.   All religion is man-made and it separates us from God. That is why I believe God hates religion.

Satan knew what God had said. He was probably present when God formed Adam and gave him this commandment. When Satan realized the Woman did not know the word of God, he uttered what the Bible later calls "The Lie." (2 Thes. 2:11) "Ye shall not surely die!...Ye shall be as gods, knowing good and evil." Satan's fall came when he chose to be his own God and he tempts man to do the same. So the woman was tempted to touch the fruit and when she did not die, she began to question God in her heart. She then took the fruit and ate it and gave it to "her husband with her and he did eat."

It is astonishing that she didn't ask her husband who was standing there and he didn't speak up. Eve was deceived by Satan and committed the first "sin of ignorance", but Adam was not deceived and committed the first "willful sin." ("Adam was not deceived"- 1 Tim. 2:14) Both Adam and Eve sinned and the glory of God departed. That's how they knew they were naked and sought to cover themselves with fig leaves.

We don't know how long after the fall of Adam and Eve God came walking in the garden, but we do know He usually met with Adam in the cool of the evening. Instead of running to Him, the couple now hid from God because for the first time they were afraid of God. Of course, God was not surprised, for He knows everything. When he called to Adam and Eve and confronted their sin, they made excuses for their sin. Man blamed the woman and the woman blamed the serpent. Not much has changed in 2000 years. God is still calling to man to come fellowship with Him and man is still hiding from God.

But did they really die? When Adam and Eve ate of this fruit, they experienced a three-fold death. The first was **Spiritual Death.** This was a separation from fellowship with God, the source of spiritual life. The second aspect of their death was **Physical Death.** This was a separation of body and soul/spirit. No one mentioned in the Bible lived for more than 1000 years of age. ("a thousand years as one day" - 2 Peter 3:8) The oldest was Methuselah who lived to be 969! (Gen. 5:27) The third aspect of death was **Eternal Death.** This is the ultimate separation from God in hell. (sheol- Rev. 20:11-15)

Most people do not know that God is "pro-choice." He created us with a "free will." We can actually choose life or death, heaven or hell, a blessing or a curse. When Adam & Eve ate of the fruit, they made the following choices:

1. **They chose to sin against God by breaking His commandment.** The Woman was tested by the serpent to determine how much she knew of the word of God. She could have turned to her husband and asked him what God really said, but she chose to eat the fruit anyway. When we are deceived, we seldom want to confront the source of the lie. Adam knew the truth, but chose his relationship with the Woman over his relationship with God. We often allow the blessing God has given us to stand in the way of our obedience to Him.

2. **They chose knowledge of good & evil over the knowledge of God.** This is perhaps the greatest tragedy of all. Our human nature wants to know everything. We want to know the how, where, when, why of life, rather than trusting God to lead and guide us.

How many times have we asked God "why" or "when" only to hear His voice saying "My grace is sufficient for thee." God does not give us knowledge of the details, but His direction. He does not tell us what and when something will happen, but to trust Him in all situations. He does not give us the mercy and grace to endure life's trials in advance, but as we pass through them. When we choose knowledge over a life of faith, we rob ourselves of knowing God and His glory. Are you seeking knowledge or are you seeking Him?

3. **They chose to be clothed with the natural rather than be clothed with the glory of God**. Ps. 34:5 seems to indicate that Adam & Eve were clothed with the glory of God. "They looked unto Him and were lightened (radiant) and their faces were not ashamed." Ps. 104:2 states "God covers Himself with "light as with a garment." On the Mount of Transfiguration, Jesus' "raiment was white as the light." (Mt. 17:2) This may be an example of what our robes of righteousness will be in heaven – pure light from the glory of God. Adam & Eve clothed themselves with fig leaves and later God clothed them with animal skins;

both natural materials. (Gen. 3:7, 21)   God's covering involved the shedding of blood.   His blood covers us from all our sins.   What does it mean to be clothed with the natural instead of the heavenly?   It means choosing the things of this world over the glory of heaven.   It means the lust of the flesh, the lust of the eye and the pride of life instead of laying up your treasures in heaven. It means choosing the world over heaven.

Religion cannot remove the effects of sin.   Only repentance and receiving the forgiveness of God can renew your relationship with Him and restore the glory of God to your life.   You do not have to go to a church building or synagogue and ask a minister for forgiveness.   You can have access to God right now where you are.   Just pray from your heart, telling God you are sorry for your sins and want forgiveness based on the life, death and resurrection of Jesus Christ, His only begotten Son.   God will forgive you, cleanse you with the blood of Jesus and change you into a new creation.

CHAPTER 5

WHAT IS THE FRUIT OF THE KNOWLEDGE OF GOOD & EVIL?

To have the knowledge of good and evil or being religious does not ensure mankind will do what he knows to be good. Man's fallen nature will always deceive and defeat him and cause him to do the opposite of what he intended to do. There is a big difference between our good intentions and good works.

Paul said in Romans 3:12, "There is none that doeth good, no not one." Also, in Romans 7:18-19, Paul stated "...for to will (to do good) is present with me; but how to perform that which is good, I find not." So if I know what is good and want to do good, how come I do evil? The reason is man's indwelling nature of sin. So, according to the Word of God, although you and I have the knowledge of good and the will to do good, we can only do evil because it is in our nature.

The problem we have is that we don't believe this to be true. We believe that we can do good. In Exodus 24:3, when Moses gave the 10 commandments to Israel ("Wherefore the Law is holy, and the commandment holy, and just, and good." –Rom 7:12), all the people of Israel said "All the words which the Lord hath said, we will do." Of course, they immediately went out and broke all of these commandments. How could they have been so deceived?

These scriptures give us some clues about man's heart:

"He feedeth on ashes; a <u>deceived heart</u> hath turned him aside, that he cannot deliver his soul, nor say is there not a lie in my right hand?" --- Isaiah 44:19

"For sin taking occasion by the commandment (of the Law), <u>deceived</u> me, and by it slew me."— Romans 7:11

"The heart is <u>deceitful</u> above all things, and desperately wicked; who can know it?"—Jer. 17:9

"But evil men and seducers shall wax worse and worse, <u>deceiving and being deceived</u>." –2 Tim. 3:13

So we see the real fruit of the knowledge of good and evil is SELF-DECEIT. We are deceived by our own hearts into thinking that if we know good from evil; if we know the Bible (commandments); if we know all the religious rules and we have the utmost desire to do the will of God, then we will be successful in doing the good and avoiding the evil. This deception is at the heart of religion. "Nothing is easier than self-deceit. For what each man wishes, that he also believes to be true." --Demosthenes

Man takes the Word of God and adds a myriad of rules and regulations until he has created an organized and planned religion, which he uses to gain God's blessings. Man chooses knowledge of religion over knowing God. The Bible says: "Knowledge puffeth up; but Love buildeth up." (1 Cor. 8:1). Religion offers knowledge, but a relationship with God offers His love.

So the sin that came on the world through Adam was not gaining the knowledge of good and evil, but by disobeying God's commandment. "Thou shalt not" still produces rebellion in most of the human race and causes us to want to do the very thing we are told not to do. Why did God test Adam with this commandment knowing he would fail? Adam was created differently than the previous created beings (angels). Adam was given a free will. He was free to choose God or not. The motivation for choosing God was not fear of His power, but the enjoyment of His love. God wanted us to love Him and have a relationship with Him.

Do you have a relationship with God? He wants you to be a part of His life. What an honor that someone so important and powerful would want you as a friend! And He has made it so simple. All you have to do is acknowledge His presence and call upon His Name. He will hear you and reach out to you. Change your mind about God and know Him as a loving Father. Acts 17:27 (NIV) says ..."God did this so that they would seek him and perhaps reach out for him and find him, though he is not far from any one of us."

CHAPTER 6

WHAT IS THE HISTORY OF RELIGION?

The Bible gives a history of man's choices and the consequences of those choices. We are shaped by our choices in life and ultimately in death. So it is with mankind today. Let's look at some of the earliest choices made by man. In this chapter, we will look at the story of Cain and Abel.

When God killed animals in Genesis 3:21 and provided "coats of skins" to cover the nakedness of Adam and Eve, He must have instructed them as to animal sacrifices and the shedding of blood for the covering of sin. Adam and Eve taught this way to their children. Abel brought the "firstlings of his flock and the fat thereof" as a sacrifice for sin. God accepted this sacrifice and consumed it by fire.

However, Cain chose to offer a different sacrifice. He offered the fruit of his labor –an offering of his crops. God did not accept Cain's sacrifice. This rejection made Cain so mad that he murdered his brother Abel. Why did this happen?

Abel was a shepherd and Cain was a farmer. It made perfect sense to Cain that offering the fruit of the ground (which was cursed by God) was to offer the sweat of his brow—a gift of himself. However, God ordained one way to forgiveness – the shedding of blood of an innocent lamb. This foretold the day when the Lamb of God would come and offer himself as the ultimate sacrifice for sin. God was not choosing Abel's "works" over Cain's "works." He was choosing Abel's obedience over Cain's disobedience. God was ordaining faith in a perfect sacrifice provided by God as the way of salvation.

God was receiving the life of the lamb instead of the death of an animal. The Old Testament saints were always reminded that these things were only "shadows" of things to come. They looked forward by faith to the coming of the Messiah, the Lamb of God, for true forgiveness. New Testament saints look back by faith to the cross where the Lamb of God was crucified and said "It is finished."

"Knowing that a man is not justified by the works of the law, but by faith…" Gal. 2:16

"The just shall live by faith." –Gal. 3:11

God has established from the beginning that to receive His forgiveness, we must rely on faith in the shed blood of the Lamb of God. We will never be justified by religion which depends on the works of man.

The following is a comparison of Abel and Cain showing the difference between the way of faith and the works of religion:

ABEL WAS …	BUT CAIN WAS ….
Keeper of sheep	Tiller of the ground
Offered a sacrifice by faith	Offered a sacrifice of works
Justified by faith	Condemned by self-deceit
Spiritual worshiper	Religious worshiper
Obedient to God – Blessed	Disobedient to God – condemned

ABEL WAS …	BUT CAIN WAS …
His business was raising sheep – life	*His business was tilling ground – cursed*
Humble – trusting God himself	*Prideful – trusting*
Walked with God	*Walked with the wicked one (1 Jn. 3:12)*
Spiritual –with power over power the devil	*Carnal – with no over the devil*
Persecuted by the religious righteous	*Persecuting the*

Are you humbly walking in obedience to God, justified by faith, or are you trusting in religious pride and condemning yourself? Are you a "Cain" or an "Abel"? Religion is more than a crutch. It is a tool of the devil. Satan uses religion to divert Christians from the true faith and uses their own carnal nature to condemn the world and everyone in it. Jesus did not come to condemn the world. He came that everyone would have a chance to meet God.

Many people I have met have been hurt by the hypocrisy and cruelty of religion. Many have honestly tried to find God inside a religious organization only to be disillusioned and discouraged. They left that "way" and began looking for love in all the wrong places. But, don't let religion stop you from finding a real relationship with God. Going to church does not make you a Christian, any more than going to a barn, makes you a horse. Find God first, and He will lead you to where He wants you to be.

There are so many different religions and denominations within each religion, that it is impossible to determine on your own what is true and what is false. God intended religion to be divided, so it would not grow to a point where it took over the world. We will see in the next chapter how God had to stop mankind from uniting in rebellion against Him during a time when all men spoke one language and had the same culture. It happened after the Flood when mankind was one family.

CHAPTER 7

WHY RELIGION IS DIVIDED WHILE THE CHURCH IS ALWAYS UNITED.

During the years I pastored a church, many efforts were put forth to unite all the churches in the area. I participated in those efforts because I thought it was a shame that so many different churches and buildings were erected (often on the same street) by different denominations when it would be simpler to build one building and share it on different days of the week. I was pretty naïve in those days. I had not read the story of the tower of Babel in Genesis Chapters 10 and 11.

Genesis 10 describes the families of Noah after the flood and their dispersion into nations. One of the descendants of Noah was Nimrod ("a mighty hunter before the LORD") and "the beginning of his kingdom was Babel." The Jewish-Roman historian Flavius Josephus, in his Antiquities of the Jews (c AD 94), recounted history as found in the Hebrew Bible and mentioned the Tower of Babel. He wrote that it was Nimrod who had the tower built and that Nimrod was a tyrant who tried to turn the people away from God.

The following is a quote from Josephus:

"Now it was Nimrod who excited them to such an affront and contempt of God. He was the grandson of Ham, the son of Noah, a bold man, and of great strength of hand. He persuaded them not to ascribe it to God, as if it were through his means they were happy, but to believe that it was their own courage which procured that happiness. He also gradually changed the government into tyranny, seeing no other way of turning men from the fear of God, but to bring them into a constant dependence on his power."

So a people who just survived a world-wide flood, decided to rebel against God and build a "flood-proof" tower and city to show their defiance.

America has not changed much from the days of Babel. After 9/11, a new "tower" was built to show America's power and defiance against what many believe was the judgment of God. An excellent book written by a messianic pastor, Jonathan Cahn, entitled "The Harbinger", tells of an attempt by this nation to defy the course of judgment, apart from repentance, and instead has set in motion a chain of events to bring about the very calamity it sought to avert. It is an excellent book and worthy of your consideration.

Genesis 11 begins with the statement "And the whole earth was of one language, and of one speech." By implication, all of the inhabitants of the earth were from the same family and had a common language, customs and religion. There are many accounts all over the world concerning the flood and the aftermath including the tower or city of Babel. Some accounts state the tower was several miles high and surpassed all other structures like the pyramids or the Aztec temples.

Ruins of the base of this tower still exists today in modern Babylon and can be seen on Google Earth. So we see this was not some barbaric civilization, but far advanced from what we have seen in other historical civilizations. "And the LORD said, Behold, the people is one, and they have all one language; and this they begin to do: and now nothing will be restrained from them, which they have imagined to do." (Genesis 11:6)

God in His mercy did not send another flood to destroy them, but caused division by confusing their language so they could not understand one another. We don't know from the biblical account if God did anything else to divide them, but we know His intention was to forever keep them from uniting in open rebellion against God. Man is still divided today by many things including language, culture, religion, etc. The only way for man to unite is through Jesus Christ our Lord where all are one in Him.

The church of Jesus Christ is one living body. Paul states in Romans 12:5, "So we, being many, are one body in Christ, and every one members one of another." The church is called "the body of Christ" in many verses of scripture.

"For as the body is one, and hath many members, and all the members of that one body, being many, are one body: so also is Christ." 1 Corinthians 12:12

"Now ye are the body of Christ, and members in particular." 1 Corinthians 12:27

"Christ is the head of the church: and he is the saviour of the body." Ephesians 5:23

"For no man ever yet hated his own flesh; but nourisheth and cherisheth it, even as the Lord the church: For we are members of his body, of his flesh, and of his bones." Ephesians 5:29-30

"This is a great mystery: but I speak concerning Christ and the church." Ephesians 5:32

So we see that we are all baptized into one body by the Holy Spirit when we receive Christ by grace through faith. This spiritual body is one and can never be divided. Religion may try to separate us into denominations and various man made doctrines, but the Church of the Living God will always be one in Christ. We will never be united by religion.

It is also interesting to note that all the things that divide men and nations today, may not be man-made. Because of the destructive nature and cruelty of man's nature, God may have divided mankind in many ways to restrain us from doing evil. We do know that true unity comes from Jesus Christ and Christianity can transcend all cultures, languages, governments and religions.

CHAPTER 8

WHAT DID JESUS HAVE TO SAY ABOUT RELIGION?

If Jesus were to walk among us in the flesh again, He would probably have a lot to say about religion. Several encounters in the gospels reveal His great hatred for religion. Jesus did not mince words or try to be polite when He was addressing the religious leaders of that day. (One of the reasons for the title of this Book is Jesus' attitude toward religion.)

Here are some examples of what Jesus spoke to the religious hypocrites of his day:

"Woe unto you, scribes and Pharisees, hypocrites!..."
"Ye compass sea and land to make one proselyte, and when he is made, ye make him twofold more the child of hell than yourselves." Matthew 23:14-16

"Ye make clean the outside of the cup and of the platter, but within they are full of extortion and excess." Matthew 23:24-26

"Ye are like unto whited sepulchers, which indeed appear beautiful outward, but are within full of dead men's bones, and of all uncleanness." Matthew 23:26-28

I don't think "hate" is too strong a word for how Jesus felt about religion. He knew how damaging and deceiving religion could be to those who were seeking God. Many will come to Christ only to fall prey to religious indoctrination and lose the joy of their salvation. Jesus warned His disciples about the false righteousness of those who promoted religion.

"For I say unto you, That except your righteousness shall exceed the righteousness of the scribes and Pharisees, ye shall in no case enter into the kingdom of heaven." Mt. 5:20   In other words, if all you have is religion, you will not make it into heaven. Pretty strong condemnation from the King of Kings and Lord of Lords!

Another way Jesus talked about religion was through parables. Parables were a simple story or word-picture that revealed truth to the common man. Jesus taught in parables to confound the wisdom of men and to speak to the humble in heart. The truths taught in these parables concerned the kingdom of heaven or this present Church Age.

The parables were called "mysteries" because they were not taught in the Old Testament. They were revealed by Christ only to those who had an intimate relationship with Him. When his disciples asked him to explain the parables, Jesus used the parable of the sower. He stated in Mark 4:13 that this parable provided a key to understanding all of the parables. Let's look at this parable.

The parable of the sower can be found in the gospels (Matthew 13, Mark 4 and Luke 8). The 12th chapter of Matthew ends with Jesus describing a new relationship - those who do the will of the Father. Chapter 13 begins "on the same day" with Jesus leaving the house (of Israel) and sitting by the seaside. As great multitudes gathered on the seashore, Jesus sat in a ship and began teaching them. The 4th chapter of Mark states Jesus "sat in the sea." The seas in the Bible can represent the vast multitudes of people in the world or nations.

As we study this parable and, later, the interpretation Jesus gives His disciples, we see it is about four kinds of people who hear the message of the gospel. First of all, the sower is <u>Christ</u> and the seed being sown is <u>the Word of God</u>. The fowls of the air are <u>Satan's demons</u>. The four kinds of ground receiving the seed are <u>four conditions of the heart</u>. Only one of the four who "hear" the word of God actually understands it, believes it and obeys it producing spiritual fruit. Billy Graham once speculated that of all those who came forth to receive Christ at his crusades, only one out of four believed unto salvation. Jesus said not everyone who professes to be a Christian is really a true convert, but those who show forth spiritual fruit. "Ye shall know them by their fruits." (Matthew 7:16).

Why didn't hearing the word of God produce faith in all of those who heard it? Because the different condition of their hearts hindered them. The four can be summarized this way:

1. **The Wayside Hearers** – Their hearts were hardened by outside influences which wore a path where nothing could grow. Satan was able to steal the word out of their hearts before it could do them any good. Many have been so offended by religion, that they remain confused about the true gospel. These hear without understanding.

2. **The Stony Hearers** - Their hearts have a thin veneer of good soil, but underneath lies a bedrock of unbelief. They want the blessings of God and are initially excited, but when true faith is required to withstand the trials and persecution that comes to all Christians, they fall away. These hear without believing.

3. **The Worldly Hearers** - These hear the word and believe, but the temptations of the world causes them to choose ambition and money over God. They say, but do not obey. They talk the talk, but do not walk the walk. These hear without obeying. Sadly, this is the most common type of believer today.

4. **The Fruitful Hearers** – These hear the word and receive it on good ground. Ground that has been plowed and pulverized – often a broken and humble heart that has experienced the brutality of the world and the sinfulness of man. These bear much fruit of the spirit such as love, joy, peace, longsuffering, gentleness, goodness, and faith.

Jesus said: "I am the vine, ye are the branches: He that abideth in me, and I in him, the same bringeth forth much fruit: for without me ye can do nothing. (John 5:15)

Additional parables were given using the same analogies. The parable of the wheat and the tares (weeds). This time the seed or word of God is sown in a field (the world) and while the sower slept (Jesus has been away for nearly 2000 years), the enemy (Satan) came and sowed counterfeit believers that bore no fruit. The false believers' hypocrisy and religion turn off the world and many do not believe the word of God.

The parable of the mustard seed is similar in that the word of God is sown and grows into a very large tree. Mark 4 says the tree "shooteth out great branches" and the "fowls of the air" come and hide in the shadows. This rapid growth of the tree which provides a haven for the demons of Satan is a picture of the rapid growth of religion which provides cover for Satan to infiltrate. It is interesting that this tree bears no fruit. Could the great branches refer to all the denominations of the Christian religion? Not all growth is of God.

Yet another parable compares the kingdom of heaven to a woman who took leaven and mixed it in three measures of wheat (flour) until all of it was leavened. In the Bible, leaven is equated with impurity and sin. The woman represents religion and the leaven false doctrine that has permeated the word of God. So many Bible versions and teachings have been corrupted, that without a close relationship with God, who knows what is real and what to believe. Truth mixed with false doctrine doesn't remain truth for very long.

"How is it that ye do not understand that I spake it not to you concerning bread, that ye should beware of the leaven of the Pharisees and of the Sadducees? Then understood they how that he bade them not beware of the leaven of bread, but of the doctrine of the Pharisees and of the Sadducees." Mt. 10:11-12

Although the religious crowd did not understand these parables, they knew to whom Jesus was talking. "And when the chief priests and Pharisees had heard his parables, they perceived that he spake of them. Mt. 21:45

CHAPTER 9

WHAT HAPPENED TO RELIGION IN THIS COUNTRY?

Do you know the history of religion in America?

As students of American history know.....it began with the Pilgrims. Who were they? The Pilgrims were Separatists, America's Calvinist Protestants, who rejected the institutional Church of England. They believed that the worship of God must originate in the inner man, and that corporate forms of worship prescribed by man interfered with the establishment of a true relationship with God. The Separatists used the term "church" to refer to the people, the Body of Christ, not to a building or institution. As their Pastor John Robinson said, "[When two or three are] gathered in the name of Christ by a covenant made to walk in all the way of God known unto them as a church ."

How did these Pilgrims become Separatists?

During the latter part of the reign of Elizabeth I of England, a small number of Christians took the doctrine of Puritanism to its logical conclusion and separated themselves from the "impure" national church to form small churches. Though never more than several hundred in numbers, they were hunted down and severely punished by the agents of Elizabeth and James I, as well as being strongly criticized by the Puritan preachers. They eventually moved to Holland to avoid persecution in 1609. A small part of the church pastored by John Robinson sailed from Holland on the Mayflower. The Mayflower landed in Plymouth, Massachusetts on November 11, 1620. Robinson never emigrated, choosing rather to remain as pastor of the major portion of the church, which stayed in Holland. Though he never arrived in New England, his influence on the Plymouth Separatists was profound, due to his teaching before the voyage and through his tracts and letters to the flock.

The church in America remained true to their Puritan roots for many years. They believed God required men to labor diligently in their callings and to improve the earth. This translated into a "protestant" work ethic that included "thrift, industry, frugality, scrupulous financial honesty, a horror of debt, and the integrity of credit" as virtues. These concepts spread to the common people and freed them from the bondage of religion. Every man had the right to his own religious views and practices. Every man could commune with God for himself. One of the most important beliefs was a conviction that the Bible contained absolutely authoritative answers to all questions of human and social action.

When did the church become an organized business?

Until the Civil War, religion was typically the matter of small-town or village dynamics led by itinerant preachers and settled pastors who formed little congregations based on styles of prayer or preaching or liturgy. Most churches did not even think of themselves as part of "denominations" until well into the nineteenth century. By the mid-twentieth century, religion was a big business, having embarked on a "period of unprecedented institutionalization" in the United States and elsewhere.

American churches were organized on the same principles and structures as were twentieth-century American corporations. Beginning around 1890, denominations built massive bureaucratic structures, modeling themselves after American businesses, complete with corporate headquarters, program divisions, professional development and marketing departments, franchises (parish churches), training centers, and career tracks. Faith increasingly became a commodity and membership rolls and money measures of success. The business of the church replaced the mission of the church.

Today the business of religion is sustained by money as are most "businesses." However, the Church of Jesus Christ was never intended to be a business. God didn't call us to be successful, but to be fruitful. True Christianity is sustained by the love of God, not money. I will discuss this more in the next chapter.

What can be done to wake up the Church in America today?

Many believe there have been four great Christian awakenings in America dating back to the 1700's. What is an "awakening"? I believe an awakening is a divine move of God to wake up His church from their slumber and to give them a true vision of the church's purpose. It is not based on our imagination and doing, but "it is the Lord's doing and it is marvelous in our eyes."(Psalm 118:23)

The Great Awakenings recorded in history were: the First Great Awakening, 1730-60; the Second Great Awakening, 1800-1830, the Third Great Awakening, 1890-1920, and the Fourth Great Awakening, 1960-1990 (Revivals, Awakenings and Reform, William McLaughlin). In my opinion, the Fourth Great Awakening began with the "Jesus Freak" movement and the outpouring of the Baptism of the Holy Ghost. This awakening led to the modern non-denominational and charismatic reforms in the Church. However, having been present during this awakening, I believe it only lasted from 1960 to 1990.

But, I believe there is yet a fifth awakening coming to America which will prepare the Bride of Christ for the Rapture and the Second Coming of Jesus Christ. This awakening will call Christians back to their first love – Jesus Christ and will be recognized by the outpouring of God's glory on the Church. Jesus Christ "will present to Himself a glorious church, not having spot or wrinkle" when He comes for His Bride. I do not see the church today as not having spot or wrinkle. Religion has invaded and contaminated the church causing it to operate as a worldly business, trying to please the world by conforming to it.

Who will take part in this Fifth Great Awakening in America?

According to Diana Butler Bass, only 1.6% of the population in the United States is atheist. Indeed, Pew's 2008 study found the "net" belief in God in the United States—adding together the 71% who are certain God exists with the 17% who hold some doubts and the 4% who have many doubts – equals 92% of the population. And that number, 92%, is historically in line with belief levels in previous generations.

The Pew study further probed toward what kind of God believers think exists. Of adults, 60% claim that God is a person "with whom people can have a relationship," while 25% define God as an impersonal force. About 7% say that God exists, but it is impossible to know anything about that God. Baylor

University researchers further explored the specific views of God that Americans now hold. They too found that roughly 92% of Americans say they believe in God. The good news is that 92% of America believes God exists. For the Bible says, "he that cometh to God must believe that HE IS." (Hebrews 11:6) (Christianity After Religion: The End of Church and the Birth of a New Spiritual Awakening, Diana Butler-Bass).

Presenting this population with the truth that God exists and wants a personal relationship with them through His Son Jesus Christ is not that big of a reach. Most Americans who have never read the Bible judge Christianity by its' religious participants and not by the true nature of Jesus Christ. When Christians remove the "religious mask" and free themselves to be what they were created to be, then the true nature of Jesus Christ will shine forth from them. Isaiah 2:1-5 MSG tells us "He'll show us the way He works so we can live the way we're made."

Is now the time for another awakening?

When God first began to deal with me about writing this book, I felt no one would want to read it. I waited and prayed for the right time to publish such a book. I knew that no prophecy or word from God was "of any private interpretation" for no prophecy ever originated because some man willed it, but men spoke from God by the Holy Spirit. And because Jesus speaks to all of His children, I waited until I heard the same message coming forth from God's people. I believe now is the time for this Great Awakening. As my friend and evangelist, Steve Sampson, told me many years ago, "The next move of God will have no religious bones in it."

In a recent book entitled "Jesus>Religion" by Jefferson Bethke, he quotes from the works of the famous German theologian Dietrich Bonhoeffer. In 1944, Bonhoeffer wrote: "We are moving towards a completely religion-less age; people as they are now simply cannot be religious anymore. Even those who honestly describe themselves as 'religious' do not in the least act up to it. So they presumably mean something quite different by 'religious.'" He too desired to get to a place of "religion-less Christianity." The next spiritual awakening will be free of religion and will cause many to come to Christ.

You may ask why is this separation from organized religion necessary. Does religion really limit the supernatural move of God?

God has always hated religion. The ancient people of Israel were rebuked for their empty religious worship. In Isaiah 1:13-17 (MSG) God says: "Quit your worship charades. I can't stand your trivial religious games; monthly conferences, weekly Sabbaths, special meetings—meetings, meetings, meetings—I can't stand one more! Meetings for this, meetings for that, I hate them! You've worn me out!"

God further said in Isaiah 1 (MSG): "I'm sick of your religion, religion, religion, while you go right on sinning. When you put on your next prayer-performance, I'll be looking the other way. No matter how long or loud or often you pray, I'll not be listening. And do you know why? Because you are tearing people to pieces, and your hands are bloody."

What a rebuke from God! Can the same words apply to organized religion today? Pray for a new awakening, not only in America, but in the world-wide Church. Pray for deliverance of the Church from religion. Satan will not easily release God's people from religious bondage. Pray to God for more Moses' to lead His people out of religion. Tell Satan "to let God's people go!"

When the Israelites were delivered from Egypt, they just walked away from it. Many of you will be walking away from religion and tradition to find you now have time for a real relationship with Jesus Christ. No more endless activities and meetings to keep you occupied and away from quiet time with Him. Prayer will become a priority and remaining in His presence a daily joy. Sinners will become attracted to you and want to be your friend because of the outflowing presence of God. Who doesn't want love, joy and peace in this chaotic world? You will completely lose your judgmental attitude and begin to love sinners the way Jesus did. You will be able to live in the world, but not be of the world. You can have contact with sinners without contamination of sin. You can finally have an influence with people in your every-day walk. This is what true Christianity is all about...the reality of Jesus Christ in a living person.

CHAPTER 10

WHAT IS THE ROLE OF MONEY IN CHRISTIANITY?

When editing this book, my wife who is already an accomplished author, warned me that this chapter was pretty "rough." She didn't mean it wasn't truthful or written poorly, but that it might offend some people. I understood what she meant right away. Money has caused more people problems in this world that just about any other thing. Money in itself is not evil, but the Bible says it is "the love of money that is the root of all evil." Most people today equate money and religion as inseparable.

When I first met Alan, the friend mentioned in Chapter One, he was a guest in our little, store-front church in Marietta, Georgia. He had recently married his wife, Mary, and moved from Texas to Georgia. As we worshipped God, I noticed that he would raise his left hand in the air to praise God, but kept the right hand behind his back. Since most of the congregation was lifting both hands, it was obvious

Alan was different. I met Alan and Mary after the service and found them to be a wonderful couple and we had a lot in common.

We invited them over to our house to eat some "Texas-style" food and to have some fellowship. After some time, I asked Alan if he had any problems with his right arm. He said, "No." He asked me why I wanted to know. I told him about the worship service and how I noticed he only worshiped with his left hand and kept his right hand behind his back. He told me that he kept his right hand over his wallet to protect it because preachers always want your money. Alan had a dry sense of humor like most Texans, but there was an element of truth to what he said.

The difference between religion and Christianity is that religion is sustained by money and Christianity is sustained by love. Religion is truly a business that cannot exist without a continuous flow of money. The religious organization and infrastructure demands money to pay for salaries, buildings to occupy and programs to entertain its audience. I have observed on many occasions that the time taken to receive an offering often exceeded the time taken to preach a sermon or for prayer. Most consider religion and money to be synonymous.

Aren't we supposed to give money to the Church?

Yes, but what the New Testament calls giving is often far different than what churches preach today. In the Old Testament, monies were collected in the Jews religion for the support of the nation and synagogue. Under the law there were many rules and regulations concerning giving to support the priesthood of the Levites and the temple. The Old Testament called these offerings "tithes." In America, we call them income taxes and charitable gifts.

However, the word "tithes" is rarely used in the New Testament to describe giving to the church or to the business of the church. God does command us to give, but we are not limited to the ten percent we commonly refer to as tithes. Paul makes it abundantly clear in the New Testament that we are no longer under the Law. "So a previous physical regulation and command is cancelled because of its weakness and ineffectiveness and uselessness – for the Law never made anything perfect." (Hebrews 7:18 AMP) It has been said that "tithes are a debt we owe, but offerings are a seed we sow" but does that saying really describe New Testament giving? Our debts under the Law are forgiven under the New Covenant.

Another offering was called the "atonement or tribute money" required for every Jewish male 20 years and older. This assessment of a half-shekel was a ransom or tax for being part of the family of God. The money was used to support the temple. In Matthew 17:24-27, Peter was asked if his Master paid "tribute" money. Peter, out of embarrassment, stated "Yes." But later Jesus confronted him about the matter and asked Peter a question. "Do the kings of the earth take custom or tribute of their own children or of strangers?" Peter answered, "Strangers." Jesus then said, "Then the children (of the King) are free."

This scripture clearly teaches that if you are a child of God, you do not have to pay God or the Church anything for your salvation. But we are commanded to give certain things to God. 1 Corinthians 8 has a lot to say about the principles and purposes of New Testament giving. It first teaches we are to give our whole beings to God. He then owns not only you, but all you have. Giving in the New Testament is to be a grace and love act to meet the needs of others. Giving to the poor was most often the reason for giving. We should take giving seriously and always pray about what and how to give.

There may come a day when the Church cannot afford the luxuries of beautiful buildings and ornate surroundings. Without the trappings of religion, many will grieve for their traditions and lost comforts. It will take more discipline on our parts to seek God and read the Bible and hear from God. We should no longer depend on someone else to tell us what God is saying. We need to hear God for ourselves. We should no longer depend on others to do all the evangelizing. We need to go out into the world and let the reality of Jesus Christ shine forth. I believe that day has arrived. The Body of Christ must rise up and be the Church. Be confident that God will order our steps and the Holy Spirit will do the work of God. We just have to pray and obey and be at the right place, at the right time to see God's glory at work.

Giving in the Bible is to be anonymous, so those who receive have no one to thank but God. The Bible states, "don't let the left hand know what the right hand is doing" and to "give in secret and God will reward us openly." Matthew 6:3-4   "Freely we have received, freely give." Matthew 10:8   I believe it is part of our individual Christian experience to get involved with the poor and to give personally, not through a large organization who consumes a large portion for administrative purposes. The day will come when the world will not associate Christianity with money.   It may be that our gifts are not currency, but a sharing of what we already have.   Peter said to the lame man at the Gate Beautiful, "Silver and gold have I none; but such as I have give I thee." (Acts 3:6 KJV) Truly in that day, we will "render unto Caesar the things that are Caesars, and to God the things that are Gods." (Matthew 22:21)

What does Jesus Christ say about money and religion?

Jesus Christ is speaking today to the church. The churches mentioned in the book of Revelation received a prophetic message from Jesus.   He told them many things, but one of the things He warned them about was the doctrine of Balaam and the doctrine of the Nicolaitans.

Jesus chastised the church in Revelation 2 when He said, "But I have a few things against you, because you have those who hold the <u>doctrine of Balaam</u>, who taught Balak to put a stumbling block before the children of Israel, to eat things sacrificed to idols, and to commit sexual immorality. [15] Thus you also have those who hold the <u>doctrine of the Nicolaitans</u>, which thing I hate."

What is the doctrine of Balaam? Balaam was a prophet who prophesied for money. Thus, his preaching, his teaching, just became a job. Why? In Balaam's case it was greed. However, in the case of the church, the need for money has grown out of an overabundance of labor and work. "The bigger the church - the larger the paid staff."

In the book <u>Christ versus Religion</u>, Witness Lee states "All those who work for the Lord should do so not for money, but out of an intimate and burning love for the Lord Himself. We should serve the Lord because His love is burning within us.... How is it that

Christianity today has become such a dreadful religion? ...Because of the matter of money..."

Inevitably following the doctrine of Balaam is the doctrine of the Nicolaitans. What is this? The word "Nicolaitan" comes from two words in Greek, *niko* and *laos*. The word *niko* means to conquer or subdue, while *laos* means people. Put together, these two words mean to subdue the people, or in other words, to control the Body of Christ. Because the service of the Lord has been commercialized, the clergy-laity system spontaneously appears. This system annuls the function of so many members and kills the Body of Christ. According to Witness Lee this is a great evil. (*Christ versus Religion,* Chapter 12, by Witness Lee)

Jesus hates the merchandizing of religion. The story of Jesus turning over the money changers tables in the Temple was an example of His anger. He said, "Take these things away! Do not make My Father's house a house of merchandise!" (Matthew 2:15)

CHAPTER 11

GOD'S JUDGMENT OF RELIGION

"For the time has come that judgement must begin at the house of God..." 1 Peter 4:17

Many know God as a heavenly Father, a God of love, a gentle, elderly type who only wants to bless you. Well, before God was Love, His name was Holy. His angels exist to guard and protect His Holiness. Nothing that defiles is allowed to come close to Him. For those of us who are guilty of sin, He is unapproachable. That is, except for His Son, Jesus Christ.

God sent His Son to live and die as a human being because He loved mankind and didn't want anyone to be sentenced to everlasting death – a death that would separate them from God for eternity. God's holiness demanded someone to live a perfect life – a life without sin. A life unto God, keeping all His commandments and doing His will. Since there was no one on earth that could meet those requirements, He came Himself in the form of a Son and fulfilled the demands of God. Then he gave Himself to die on a cross in exchange for our sins so we too might be able to meet God's holy demands.

For he hath made him to be **sin** for us, who knew no **sin**; that we might be made the righteousness of God in him. (2 Corinthians 5:21 KJV)

Likewise reckon ye also yourselves to be dead indeed unto **sin**, but alive unto God through Jesus Christ our Lord. (Romans 6:11 KJV)

So the **blood of Jesus** changed God's throne from a judgment seat to a mercy (grace) seat where God can look upon Jesus and all those who have received Him by faith as righteous and holy. God is not mad at you anymore because, as a Christian, you are hidden in Christ and have access to our father God.

Let us therefore **come boldly** unto the throne of grace that we may obtain mercy, and find grace to help in time of need. (Hebrews 4:15-16 KJV)

As good as that news is, many will not surrender to Christ and will fall under God's judgment. That includes all the world's systems and demonically inspired programs like religion. I believe that judgment has already begun in America. I believe it began in the year 2000.

Since 2000, survey data shows as much as a 12 point drop in public trust in religious institutions, with only about 20% of Americans saying they have a "great deal" of confidence in "organized religion."

This loss of trust was caused in part by five major judgments in the decade from 2000 to 2010. Several tragedies and scandals occurred which has driven many from organized religion and the houses of God. This decade has been described by Diana Butler Bass as "The Horrible Decade for Religion." Here is a summary of what happened in that decade:

2000-2010: The Horrible Decade for Religion

2001: September 11th terrorist attack: After this tragedy, thousands of Americans sought answers by seeking religion, only to find out that religion did not have the answers.

2002: Roman Catholic sex abuse scandal: After decades of sexual abuse by priests was exposed, the Roman Catholic Church was more interested in public relations control and buying their way out of the problem than fixing the problem. Nothing related to the root of the problem, such as celibacy, was changed in the church.

2003: Protestant conflict over homosexuality: The divide over showing compassion for sinners and adopting the world's standards of political correctness has split several denominations. We are called to love the sinner and not the sin. The Bible says that love "covers" (causes us to forgive and disregard) a multitude of sins. 1 Peter 4:8

2004: Death or fall of the Religious Right: The leaders of the so-called Religious Right promoted the mistaken idea that getting involved in politics would bring moral change in this country. Politics is not the way to moral change. As it has been said, "You can't legislate morality." Our founding fathers stated that without a godly constituency, our form of government would not stand. Morality among the citizens results in less government, which is always good government. This idea failed leaving many disillusioned.

2007: Great Religious Recession: Many churches have declared bankruptcy and/or lost their properties because of a sudden loss of cash flow or mismanagement of church funds. According to a Giving USA report, American individuals, groups, foundations and corporations gave $335 billion to charities in 2013 — a 3% increase from 2012 (adjusted for inflation). However, religious groups saw donations drop 1.6% from 2012 to 2013. This is compared to a 6-7% increase in giving to the arts, education and the environment.

In the United States, somewhere in the range of 25% to 30% of the population under the age of 30 neither attends religious services nor have any religious preference, although about half of the unaffiliated group still says that they believe in God or understand themselves to be spiritual. Somewhere these young adults have evidently heard that Christianity is supposed to be about love, forgiveness, and practicing what Jesus preached and that faith should give meaning to real life. They obviously are judging Christianity on its own teachings and believe the American churches come up short. The sad news is that for many churches, they are right.

WHAT ARE THE MODERN TRENDS
IN AMERICA CONCERNING RELIGION?

In recent decades, religious pollsters in a number of countries have begun to ask a simple question: "Do you think of yourself as.....

1. Spiritual, but not religious,
2. Religious, but not spiritual,
3. Religious and spiritual, or
4. Not spiritual and not religious?"

The results have been both surprising and steady. In the United States, some 30% of adults consider themselves "spiritual, but not religious." In 2009, Princeton Survey Research Associates found that only 9% of Americans consider themselves "religious but not spiritual" and some 48% try to combine the two into "religious and spiritual." Whatever the exact number, the trend seems clear enough in a variety of polls across the world that the word "spiritual" is a far more appealing term than "religious."

Diana Butler Bass conducted several studies over the course of 18 months where she asked several groups to do a word association using the words "spiritual" and "religious." No matter the region or denomination, all of the groups associated spirituality with experience and religion with institutions. A word association game is not a controlled, scientific study, but it is a quick gauge of current trends in what people believe. Today, people have generally substituted the word "religion" for institutional religion and "spirituality" for lively faith.

In 1999, before the "Horrible Decade for Religion," Gallup polled Americans asking whether people understood themselves to be spiritual or religious. At that time, people answered as follows:

- Spiritual only – 30%
- Religious only – 54%
- Both Spiritual and Religious – 6%
- Neither Spiritual or Religious – 9%

However, in just ten years after this poll, people responded to the same question as follows:

- Spiritual only – 30%
- Religious only – 9%

- Both Spiritual and Religious – 48%
- Neither Spiritual or Religious – 9%

Notice the shift from 1999 to 2009, those who claimed to be "religious only" dropped significantly and those who were "both spiritual and religious" jumped. The key to this change was what I believe to be God's judgment of religion in America. People became ashamed to be called religious and would tell their secular friends they were "spiritual." They still went to church, but something had changed. They were not satisfied with the status quo. They longed for a deeper spiritual experience with God.

"Holy Discontent" is a term I use to describe when God is stirring our hearts to leave our complacency and our comfort zone and launch out into deeper waters. It often expresses itself in frustration or sadness until we realize God has something much greater in store. All the great awakenings and reforms of the past began with discontent. Many Americans are expressing their discontent with organized religion and their hope that somehow the Church might regain its true bearings in the Spirit.

It is time for the Church to move away from all the hype and gimmicks used by religion today. Changing our methods to accommodate the world will only result in a worldly church. Using mass marketing to determine the needs of the unchurched and then giving them what they want may increase the numbers of people attending (and giving) to church organizations, but will not produce a spiritually mature church. Not all growth is from God. It is possible to compromise the message of Christ and create a large growing organization without any spiritual fruit and full of unethical people.

CHAPTER 12

RELIGION-LESS CHRISTIANITY

How then shall we live a Christian life without religion?   This is the question I want to pose to you. Maybe you have served religion all your life and are fully indoctrinated in the practices, traditions and beliefs of your religion.   Maybe you walked away from religion a long time ago and have not sought to have anything to do with God since that time.   God is speaking to your hearts right now.

The first step toward God is to believe He exists and wants a relationship with you.   Yes, you are unworthy and your sin has separated you from Him, but He loved you enough to take care of that problem.   He exchanged the sin-less life of Jesus Christ for your life, so you could stand perfect before Him and have real fellowship.

So there are no longer any barriers to you meeting Him and getting to know Him.   And who wouldn't want to meet the King of the Universe?   God is not asking for your money or anything you own. He really just wants you. It is that simple.

STEPS IN THE RIGHT DIRECTION

1. **Hear God's voice for yourself.** "It is written (in the Bible), Man shall not live by bread alone, but by every word that proceeds out of the mouth of God." (Matthew 4:4) Hearing God's voice daily is all the spiritual nourishment you need to know Him. Without religion, you will no longer need a man to tell you what God says. Many new Christians find it confusing when they first go to religion, because what God is telling them conflicts with what religion is telling them. They often defer to some experienced religious person, because they are unsure of themselves. Before long, religion's voice drowns out what God is saying. Hear God for yourself and you will never be deceived. "Let God be true, and every man a liar." (Romans 3:4)

How do you overcome that uncertainty that God is really speaking to you? Believe what God says about you. He said, "My sheep hear my voice, and I know them, and they follow me." (John 10:27)   Jesus Christ is not only the Good Shepherd, but he is a 24/7 Pastor to his believers. He will not only talk to you, but He will confirm His words with signs and wonders.   He knows our uneasiness and doubts and He knows how to show you it is really Him speaking. While reading the Bible or talking to a friend, the very words you thought you heard will get repeated or highlighted, so you will be in awe and amazed that God really is talking to you.

2. **Spend time alone with Him**.   There are so many loud noises and voices trying to drown out God's voice today.   It is important to find a quiet place where you can meditate on Him.   "Be still, and know...(Psalm 46:10)   This may be harder than you think, but it is worth the effort.   Prayer is not some religious exercise where we count beads or recite memorized words. Prayer is a conversation with God.   It involves listening as well as speaking. Give God a chance to get a word in the conversation.   Once you get into the practice, your heart and God's heart will communicate freely.

Christians were given a wonderful gift on the day of Pentecost when their tongues were set on fire by the Holy Ghost. They were able to talk to God in a heavenly language that Paul the Apostle called the "tongues of angels." The Holy Ghost would move their tongues and give them utterances that prayed exactly what God wanted. They prayed God's will for this earth and though they didn't understand, their spirts spoke powerful and anointed prayers. This gift is available to all Christians today and allows us to pray way beyond our natural means.

3. **Act on what God is telling you.** Walk in the direction He is showing you. Don't wait for a lot of details, just begin walking in the general direction He shows you. He will cause your path to cross others who either need to hear from you or you need to hear from them. "Your steps are ordered of the Lord". Psalms 37:23   There are no coincidences with God. Much of the ministry Jesus did was one-on-one interactions with people He met along the way. You will be surprised where God will take you.

A man named Arthur Blessitt was preaching in Hollywood, CA when God told him to take a wooden cross down off the wall and carry it. Arthur took the large cross from the wall and walked out onto Sunset Strip. After he obeyed God, God told him to walk across the city, then the state and finally the world. Arthur later stated that had he known what God intended, he would have placed a much smaller cross on the wall. As we obey God, we will travel further and have a greater sphere of influence than we ever thought possible. "And thine ears shall hear a word behind thee, saying, This is the way, walk ye in it, when ye turn to the right hand, and when ye turn to the left."...(Isaiah 30:21)

4. **Read His Testimony better known as the Bible.** The only way to understand the Bible is to let the author read it to you. The Spirit of Christ is also called the Holy Spirit. When you invite the Holy Spirit to come and live on the inside of you, you will have a perfect tutor to teach you everything Christ has said. The Bible is transformed from a "dead letter" to a "living word." You can receive personal direction for every circumstance through the process of spirit-inspired reading of the Bible.

We aren't called to worship the Bible and put it ahead of our intimate fellowship with Christ. We aren't given the Bible to increase our knowledge of the scriptures, but to receive supernatural revelation of who Christ is and what He is doing right now. The Holy Spirit and the Bible will be two witnesses to you so you can have confirmation of what God is telling you.

When I was in college, I began seeking God. I returned to organized religion hoping to find the reality of Jesus Christ for my life. I attended meetings and asked a lot of questions, but got no real answers. I waited one morning in the hallway for the pastor to walk by so I could get a word with him. I asked him this question...."You preach about the Christ who lived 2000 years ago and the One who is coming in the future, but where is Christ right now!"

The pastor seemed startled at my question and the passion with which I confronted him. He quickly fell back on his training in psychology and began answering my questions with more questions. I quickly realized he did not know the answer. This was the pastor of the largest church in town. If he didn't have a relationship with Jesus Christ, how could I have one?

Much later, I realized that anyone who has received Christ's gift of grace knows the answer to that question. Jesus Christ is alive and His presence is here on Earth. His Spirit is living inside of you right now. We can enjoy His presence now and when He comes again, we can be with Him for eternity.

Don't let religion or non-believers talk you out of this wonderful gift. It is a "personal" relationship and is not their business. All arguments cease when you meet the real person of Jesus Christ. You may not know all the answers, but you will know **He is the Answer**. Don't throw this gift away or let someone steal it from you.

My prayer and hope is that this small book has opened your eyes to the falsehood of religion and to the opportunity to know God freely and completely. Feel free to contact me if you have questions or need encouragement. My email address can be found on the back of this book.

May God set you free from all bondage and give you an exciting and blessed life!

RELIGION

By M. T. Tombs

There is an evil in the land
I see it now on every hand.
A force so strong it tears the soul
Destruction is its' ultimate goal.

It turns your focus from things above
And slowly drains you of all your love.
And full of stress, you lose your hope,
And then, my friend, you cannot cope.

Don't look to man, God alone is sincere.
He has not given us a spirit of fear,
But of love and power and a sound mind.
So boldly tell Satan "get thee behind."

Go daily to prayer, plunge deep in the Word
Until you're sure from God you have heard.
Then quickly take your stand on the wall,
And watch, wait and listen for His call.

You're needed there to warn all the others,
Religion will kill your sisters and brothers.
It appears to be a place of great acclaim,
But within is only destruction and shame.

As it is written in chapter 3 of Revelation,
The church, Laodicea, so full of elation
So fast-growing, so rich and first rate,
You do not know of your terrible fate.

You are naked, miserable and blind,
If you continue, you'll be left behind,
In the Rapture, Jesus comes for a people
Not a successful business under a steeple.

REFERENCES

1. **The Holy Bible** – King James Version (KJV), The Amplified Bible(AMP), The Message (MSG) and The New International Version (NIV)

2. Flavius Josephus, **Antiquities of the Jews** (c AD 94)

3. Jonathan Cahn, **The Harbinger**

4. William McLaughlin, **Revivals, Awakenings and Reform**

5. Diana Butler-Bass, **Christianity After Religion: The End of Church and the Birth of a New Spiritual Awakening**

6. Jefferson Bethke, **Jesus>Religion**

7. Witness Lee, **Christ versus Religion**

Notes: Several of the teachings in this book have been collected over many years of ministry. If I have failed to recognize the original authors or books from which these lessons are based please let me know.

G. T. Harpazo can be contacted
Through email at:

graceandgloryPublishing@gmail.com

Printed in Great Britain
by Amazon.co.uk, Ltd.,
Marston Gate.